The God Who Sees Me

Single Moms of the Bible and their

Lessons for Today

Colombel Publishing

The God Who Sees Me

Single Moms of the Bible and their

Lessons for today

Stephane Paul

ISBN:0692694558
ISBN-13:978-0692694558

DEDICATION

To single moms around the globe God hears our
prayers

CONTENTS

Acknowledgments

ACKNOWLEDGMENTS

This book is dedicated first to the greatest love of my
life Jesus Christ; I am so privileged that He called me into a
relationship with him. I had no idea of my worth until He
appeared in my life. To my second greatest love Christophe,
without you, I would never have known purpose. Thanks to
my wonderful family, specifically Solange and Marguerite,
who never let a day go by without encouraging me. Finally,
I am grateful to the pastors whose congregations I've quiet-
ly sat in absorbing life changing teachings & principles. Dr.
Charles Stanley, Pastor Gary Zarlengo and Pastor A.R.
Bernard, you have no idea, how you've impacted my life.

In The Beginning

Discovering Single Moms in the Bible

"Your child is in private school?" she asked incredulously. Without giving me a moment to respond, she went further, "How can you afford that? You're a single mother." Needless to say, I was taken aback. Her words stung. Was my status as a single mom an indictment which would sentence my child and me to a life of paucity? I wouldn't have been struck so hard by her words had they not come from a fellow Christian woman. I'd taken for granted that because we attended the same church, we believed in the same merciful and limitless God. It didn't occur to me that we experienced the Lord differently.

Looking back, I can't say that she intentionally meant to be harsh, but those words bruised nonetheless and stayed with me for a long time. It wasn't a surprise to me that I was a single mother. I simply didn't expect that other Christians would view me through the lens of low expectation because of it. Perhaps I was naive or lived in a bubble, but since I was in Christ, I believed that I was a new creature and the old had passed away. God was giving me a fresh start. It never dawned on me that I would be limited in any way. Since becoming a single mother, I'd experienced God's generosity. We enjoyed a good life that wasn't a result of me being a super driven career woman, nor were we even the recipients of massive child support payments. We were just living on God's grace.

I remember when the enormity of single motherhood hit me; I'd spent weeks on end crying and wondering how it would all work out. Throughout the entire ordeal, I'd read my Bible daily and prayed, but I never spoke to Him expressly about my single parent status. I kept that part of my life separate, focusing on general concerns such as increasing clients and requesting guidance in work related matters. I believed that I was the cause of my circumstances, and it was up to me to figure it out. Thankfully, the Lord interceded and stopped me from torturing myself.

One day as I sat before Him to pray during our morning meeting, the pages of my Bible fluttered to a passage that read, "I will take care of the child." It would be great if I could just tell you the chapter and verse where these words could be found, but since that day, I never found them again. All I know is that when I got up that day from our time together, I was filled with a sense of peace and an assurance that the Lord would take care of it all. True to His word throughout the many phases of my child's life, the Lord has always taken care of it all.

Over the years, that lady wasn't the only person to remark on our ability to enjoy activities that would seem out of the norm for a single mother.

On the occasions that I sought out activities for single mothers and their families, I became aware of conversations that seemed to affirm the notion that we were somehow experiencing lack. Some of my counterparts would sometimes comment on their inability to provide basic needs and satisfying experiences for their children because they were single mothers. Whenever this would happen, I wondered why God was being so nice to us. I think a little pride must have gotten in because I secretly began to think that maybe He loved us a bit more. God shook that thought out of me and reminded me that it had nothing to do with me, but everything to do with Him and how He longed for us to depend on Him.

In time, the Lord guided me toward Genesis, and in particular, the chapters that included the account of Abraham's life. I must say it was no easy task getting me to go to Genesis. Earlier in my Christian life, I began reading Genesis in the King James Version and found it to be difficult to get through. Like most Christians, I admired the great faith that Abraham demonstrated throughout his life, but I couldn't imagine that there was anything contained within his story that would have any bearing on my single mom life.

The Lord persisted and insisted on my reading Genesis 12. Eventually, He won. During our quiet time together, I grudgingly opened my Bible and began reading. When I arrived at chapter 21, I nearly fell over backward. Imagine my surprise when I came face-to-face with the Bible's first single mother. All of these years, I'd never thought that single mothers were included in the Bible, yet there was Hagar, a woman embroiled in a very messy relationship who was unceremoniously thrown into the realm of single motherhood.

Once I had the introduction to Hagar, the Lord began to take me to other entries in the Bible where I could find stories about other single mothers. I noticed that with each woman, the interaction was different and revealed specific solutions for the issues in the lives of women raising children alone. As I began to review these single mom case studies, I discovered that they often touched on very real challenges that single mothers face today, which included coping with little or non-existent child support, sustained provision, debt, tithing, the future of our offspring and much more. I slowly realized that in a sense we weren't single, because once we sought His help, the Lord was prepared to step into the role of father, husband, protector and provider as stated in Psalm 68:5 and Isaiah 54:5.

> A father of the fatherless, a defender of the widows, Is God in His holy habitation. (Psalm 68:5 WEB)

> "For your Maker is your husband,
> The LORD of hosts is His name; And your Redeemer is the Holy One of Israel; He is called the God of the whole earth." (Isaiah 54:5 NKJV)

Pairing the Lord with single mothers, to some, may seem blasphemous, after all single motherhood is not the ideal. The evidence of Gods love and mercy specifically toward single mothers in the stories we will look at can not be overlooked. Finding meaning in the interactions the Lord had with the single mothers of the Bible doesn't require a stretch of the imagination nor suspense of disbelief. I believe that the Lord purposefully put stories of single mothers in the Bible to give strength and courage to those of us who would be raising children alone.

Am I declaring that God endorses single motherhood? Not at all, but if we believe in an omnipotent and omniscient God, a future that included women raising children alone would be of no surprise to Him. The Fall affected every aspect of humanity everything was thrown out of balance—our relationship with our Maker, the environment, and each other. In His omniscience, He foresaw the implications of Adam and Eve's disobedience, having realized that all aspects of the family dynamic would suffer. A myriad of issues would arise, including that of children being raised in the absence of fathers.

When God created man and instituted the marriage relationship shared between Adam and Eve, the intention was for the man to head the household and lead the family. He would teach daughters how they should be treated and young men how to provide and protect their families. In a modern age where more than half of the households are lacking fathers and husbands, the Lord couldn't simply leave the children behind and lose entire generations. The world couldn't afford to miss out on brain surgeons, scientists, inventors, musicians, ministry servants, evangelists, poets, writers, and technology geniuses simply because they came from a single parent household. Arrangements would have to be made to save these children and lead them to the Lord's desired end.

In the same way, as Moses was leading the children of Israel out of Egypt and into their promise land, there was a transfer of power due to disobedience. If you are familiar with the Bible, you'll remember that God gave Moses a duty to lead the children of Israel to their destiny. Along the way, frustration got the better of him, and Moses disobeyed God, which precluded him from fulfilling his God-given mission. God didn't abandon His plans nor turn His back on a whole new generation because of Moses's inability to complete the task. The Lord instead raised a new leader, provided him a path, impressed upon him the need to rely on Him, and admonished him to be strong and courageous throughout the journey.

"Be strong and courageous, for you are the one who will lead these people to possess all the land I swore to their ancestors I would give them." (Joshua 1:6 NLT)

"Haven't I commanded you? Be strong and courageous. Don't be afraid. Don't be dismayed, for Yahweh your God is with you where ever you go." (Joshua 1:9 WEB)

Only be strong and courageous! (Joshua 1:18WEB)

Single mothers are the Joshua's of their families today. Due to disobedience or ignorance of the Lord's word, the intended leaders—fathers—aren't present in many households. Mothers are now being tasked with leading the children through the proverbial wilderness into the promise land of the ordained futures that God has prepared. For us to successfully arrive at our journey's end, much like what He did for Joshua, God has set for us models in the Bible; these are women who have faced and conquered many of the same challenges we face today. We are afforded a roadmap that is specific to what we all contend with at some point during our journey.

It doesn't matter, therefore, how we become single mothers, be it through an unmarried relationship, divorce, or death, the challenges are generally the same. We all face issues concerning financial security, fatigue from the weight of doing the job of two, worry over our children's emotional well-being if the father is not adequately present in their lives, etc. There is also, the added concern of external factors such as the media's negative statistics that are quick to pronounce bleak futures for children from single parent homes. In addition, let's not forget the expectation of mediocrity from well-intentioned onlookers.

The good news, however, is that Jesus Christ can answer each and every one of our concerns and meet all of our needs. God hid in plain sight throughout the Bible, beginning at Genesis, specific instances of His commitment and love for single moms. I want to make sure that every woman raising children alone knows that God is aware of our status, and He is with us just as He was with Joshua as he guided a new generation through the wilderness. By looking at the Lord's relationships with our single mom predecessors, we can understand that we don't have to go through life alone and struggle unnecessarily. Through their stories, He sends us a message that we need to rely on Him as our husband, children's father, and provider. As we will see in the narratives of Hagar, the widow of Zarephath, and the widow with the oil, there is no challenge that is too great for the Lord to handle. Their stories will inform us on how to lead a full, abundant life in Christ.

Hagar

The Bibles First Single Mother

I'd been a Christian single mother for almost eight years before I realized that there were women just like me in the Bible. In the midst of a study about Abraham, my eyes were opened, and I recognized Hagar as the first single mother in Scripture. It wasn't the first time that I'd come across her, but I never actually saw her in the context of a single mother. Every time I turned to the account of Abraham, my focus was on his great faith, the miracle of motherhood bestowed upon

13

his elderly wife Sarah, and, most importantly, his title as a friend of God. Hagar, for the most part, had always been more of a shadowy character and one that most of my studies had paid very little attention.

Once I saw Hagar as a fellow single mother, I began to ponder over the two short chapters of Genesis 16 and 21, which provided glimpses into her life. I was interested to see if her life could have any bearing on mine today and, more importantly, how the Lord reacted to her and her situation. What I discovered was a woman's story that was very relevant to mine, and her interactions with the Lord gave me an even deeper appreciation and love for Him. Just her mere presence afforded me a sense of comfort because I'd been carrying a certain level of unease about my status as a single mother, especially in church settings.

Over the years as the term single mother gained increasing use, it seemed as if it was being touted as a modern phenomena and threat to modern society. Whenever I heard the words "single mother," the images that almost always came to mind were that of poor performance, lack, struggle, and limits. I was very concerned that these external perceptions would find their way into my consciousness because I believed that this thought could have a potentially devastating impact on how we single moms saw ourselves and, more importantly, the opportunities that our children could experience.

Needless to say, when I found Hagar placed not only at the beginning of the Bible but also entwined within the narrative of a biblical hero as great as Abraham, it was a huge relief to me. Like everyone else's story in the Bible, we were just another aspect of the human story. Single mother, all of a sudden, stopped carrying the stigma of modern phenomena and a catalyst of societal downfall and was now put in the perspective of a humanity issue. Simultaneously, the words of Ecclesiastes 1:9 came to mind; there is nothing new under the sun. Never was there a time in human history since The Fall where everyone was perfect and lived perfect lives.

As I continued to examine the account of Hagar, I was excited to find other life-changing truths that offered a biblical perspective to managing the modern single parent life, but before I can share them, it's important to put her in context. Since Hagar's story is interwoven within Abraham's narrative, a quick look at his backstory will help us arrive at how she came to be. I also need to mention that throughout this book, you'll notice that I use the names Abraham and Sarah, but these names are not technically used until Genesis 17 when God renames the couple. Previously Abraham was known as Abram, but the name translates into "exalted father" while his wife Sarai becomes Sarah or "princess."

Abraham's story begins in Genesis 12; he was a man indistinguishable from any other living at that time, with the exception that God invited him to go on a journey with no destination or end. Abraham accepted leaving his home, friends, and relatives to start a new life somewhere unknown to him because of his trust in God. He embarked on a very rich adventure with the Lord, which included an escapade through Egypt and a death-defying rescue of his nephew Lot from the infamous

Sodom and Gomorrah. In time, Abraham became a wealthy man, and his obedience and faith led him to develop a very intimate relationship with the Lord.

Though Abraham seems to have it all, there is something missing; he and his wife don't have any children. One day, during one of his encounters with God, Abraham revealed his feelings about being childless. The Lord responded to him, as seen in Genesis 15:2-5, promising Abraham not only an heir but also descendants that will be too numerous to count. To make His point clear, the Lord drew Abraham's attention toward the night sky and compared the stars to the number of his descendants.

"Sovereign Lord, what can you give me since I remain childless and the one who will inherit my estate is Eliezer of Damascus?" And Abram said, "You have given me no children; so a servant in my household will be my heir."

Then the word of the Lord came to him:

"This man will not be your heir, but a son who is your own flesh and blood will be your heir." He took him outside and said, "Look up at the sky and count the stars— if indeed you can count them." Then he said to him, "So shall your offspring be." (Genesis 15:2-5 NIV)

During the time of this conversation, the Bible records Abraham's age as well beyond his seventies and his wife, Sarah way past the child bearing years. When she heard the prophecy she couldn't fathom the reality of her being a mother. She thought within her that if Abraham were going to have an heir, she wouldn't be the vehicle by which this blessed experience would occur. After contemplating the idea for a time, Sarah devised a plan for her husband to have a child. She persuaded him to sleep with Hagar, her young Egyptian maidservant, so as to usher in the fulfillment of God's prophecy.

Earlier I'd mentioned that they journeyed through Egypt, and it must have been where the couple either employed, purchased, or received

Hagar as a gift. The Bible doesn't mention how much time it took to convince Abraham to get involved with Hagar, but we know that the young woman became pregnant. Once it was confirmed that Hagar was with child, the dynamic between the two women took a dramatic turn for the worst.

In those days, a woman's greatest accomplishment was to bear children and, more importantly, an heir to her husband. Sarah had failed to accomplish this; at seventy-five, she had never been able to get pregnant. As Hagar's belly began to protrude, Sarah might have been reminded of her inadequacy and began to visit her resentment upon the younger woman.

Hagar, on the other hand, went through an enormous change in social status, from a maidservant to the wife or concubine of a very powerful man. Her head might have begun to swell with pride and she may have entertained ideas of usurping the old, barren woman. A quick look at Genesis 16:4-6 sheds some light on their domestic situation.

When she knew she was pregnant, she

began to despise her mistress. Then Sarai said to Abram, "You are responsible for the wrong I am suffering. I put my slave in your arms, and now that she knows she is pregnant, she despises me. May the Lord judge between you and me."

"Your slave is in your hands," Abram said. "Do with her whatever you think best." Then Sarai mistreated Hagar; so she fled from her. (Genesis 16:4-6 NIV)

Despite the fact that Hagar was pregnant with Abraham's only child, Sarah did not lose her position over the household. Older and wiser, she had the upper hand, which she exercised severely and began to mistreat the girl. Perhaps she became overly critical and verbally abusive, finding something wrong with Hagar's every action or word. As a result, the Bible states that Hagar ran away from home and had her first encounter with a messenger of God (Genesis 16:7-11 and 13-15NLT).

The angel of the Lord found Hagar beside a spring of water in the wilderness, along the road to Shur. The angel said to her, "Hagar, Sarai's servant, where have you come from, and where are you going?"

"I'm running away from my mistress, Sarai," she replied.

The angel of the Lord said to her, "Return to your mistress, and submit to her authority." Then he added, "I will give you more descendants than you can count."And the angel also said, "You are now pregnant and will give birth to a son. You are to name him Ishmael (which means 'God hears'), for the Lord has heard your cry of distress. (Genesis 16:7-11 NLT)

She gave this name to the Lord who spoke to her: "You are the God who sees me," for she said, "I have now seen the One who sees me." That is why the well was called Beer Lahai Roid ; it is still there, between Kadesh and Bered.

So Hagar bore Abram a son, and Abram gave

the name Ishmael to the son she had borne.
Abram was eighty-six years old when Hagar
bore him Ishmael. (Genesis 16:13-15 NLT)

At the angel's urging, Hagar returned to the
camp, but this in no way put an end to the "fight-
ing" between the two women. Later at God's ap-
pointed time, Sarah became pregnant. She received
the ability to give birth, and this erased the years
of shame that must have plagued her. No longer
would she have to bear the humiliation of barren-
ness or the insult of her insolent maiden now
turned rival. The fact that both women had born
children to the same powerful man did nothing to
quell the animosity between the two. Fully restored
Sarah must have been looking for a way to get rid
of the younger Hagar and threat to her son's in-
heritance. One day during her child Isaac's circumcision ceremony an argument erupts and gives
Sarah the excuse she needed to get rid of the two.

> Therefore she said to Abraham, "Cast
> out this servant and her son! For the
> son of this servant will not be heir with

my son, Isaac." (Genesis 21:10 WEB)

> Abraham rose up early in the morning,
> and took bread and a container of water,
> and gave it to Hagar, putting it on her
> shoulder; and gave her the child, and
> sent her away. She departed, and wan-
> dered in the wilderness of Beersheba.
> (Genesis 21:14 WEB)

Once Hagar walked out of the camp and
Abraham relinquished his fatherly responsibility
for the child, she officially became a single mother. Unlike the other single mothers we will read
about later, Hagar is the only one with whom we
get an entire glimpse of the single motherhood
journey. We see her at the threshold of single
motherhood, her challenges on the journey and
also a glimpse of her child's future. She is also
the only character whose marital status is am-
biguous. The fact that we are not clear as to
whether or not she was married to Abraham
makes her relatable to both divorced women and
mothers never married. The beginning scenes of
Hagar's new life as a single mother are as raw and

packed with emotions as any contemporary breakup would be for both mother and child. In the next section, we will conclude the verses that make up Hagar's story and look at the modern implications on the single mom life in the areas of child support, God's approach to children from single parent homes, and His provision.

Into the Wild

Then he sent her away with their son, and she wandered aimlessly in the wilderness of Beersheba.

When the water was gone, she put the boy in the shade of a bush. Then she went and sat down by herself about a hundred yards away. "I don't want to watch the boy die," she said, as she burst into tears.

But God heard the boy crying, and the angel of God called to Hagar from heaven, "Hagar, what's wrong? Do not be afraid! God has heard the boy crying as he lies there. Go to him and comfort him, for I will make a great nation from his descendants."

Then God opened Hagar's eyes, and she saw a well full of water. She quickly filled her water container and gave the boy a drink.

And God was with the boy as he grew up in the wilderness. He became a skillful archer, and he settled in the wilderness of Paran. His mother arranged for him to marry a woman from the land of Egypt. (Genesis 21:14-21 NLT)

Hagar's first few steps into single motherhood proved to be difficult. The Bible mentions that she wandered through the wilderness, lost and unable to make any headway. As Abraham handed to her the meager provisions he had packed for her, she must have been in a state of shock. Though their family had been dysfunctional and experienced many fights and disagreements, I am sure she never imagined that this would be the end result. In an instant, the young mother was cut off from all that she had come to know over the last few years. The community and family that once surrounded her were gone. Walking away from the camp, she was brokenhearted and in tears at having been so unceremoniously tossed aside like a tool that had lost its purpose. The once precious son that she'd born had suffered the same fate, going from being a cherished heir to a rejected offspring.

This Ishmael standing next to her was no small boy holding on to his mother's skirts and subject to her interpretation of the morning's events. He was a young man somewhere between the ages of thirteen and fifteen. Earlier in Genesis 17:23-27, God made a covenant with Abraham and required that every male in his household be circumcised, and at the time of the circumcision ceremony, Ishmael was already thirteen years of age. I am not sure how much time elapsed between that event and being thrown out of the camp, but what's clear is that Ishmael was a teenager.

As a young man, there was no way for him to miss the significance of his father throwing him out nor the strong feelings that would be engendered as a result. Child psychologists often state that children tend to blame themselves whenever there is a problem in the family; Ishmael must have been no different. It's not hard to imagine that he tortured himself, wondering how he could have been a better son or what he could have done to keep his family together. He must have gone through a range of emotions from abject sorrow to anger as he contemplated his father's rejection of his mother and him, all in a bid to keep the newer child.

Walking through the wilderness, his slender frame must have convulsed with tears while he lumbered under the hot sun aimlessly. Overcome by grief, pain, and a lack of water, the young man is described as almost near death. Witnessing her child's agony, Hagar placed his dehydrated body under the shade of a tree, unable to bear the sight of his imminent death. Distraught and disoriented, she couldn't assist him, she couldn't lead him out of that miserable situation, and she couldn't provide for his basic needs.

For many single mothers, we may not have had such a dramatic entry into the single mom journey, but several of us can relate to many aspects of Hagar's life. For the recently divorced woman, the displacement and loss of community that Hagar suffered is easily recognizable. The friends and family support that was created by the marriage in some cases dissolved during the process of divorce. Friends and family take sides, and as a result, an awkwardness pervades and relationships become broken or strained. Likewise, the unwed mother can also identify with Hagar's feelings of abandonment and the loss of what could have been as well as the incredulity of a man walking away from his child.

In my life and in speaking to other single mothers, a lot of us shed tears and wondered how we were going to make it through. In the years to come we would now be singularly managing a role built for two. In the case of messy divorces or a break up which resulted in a separation of father from child, we were also having to manage the range of feelings that our children would undergo. In some cases we would have to watch in helpless silence the effects of broken promises or the sheer absence of the other parent on our children's emotional state. Needless to say every single mother has a different story and some aspects of her journey will be relevant at different times of our lives.

The wilderness that Hagar's trudged through in the story is a physical and literal space. Single mothers today don't have that same physical challenge, but when you take into consideration the expanse from childhood to adulthood, it can be looked in much the same light. In the midst of the two states, there are a slew of hurdles and hormonal obstacles that must be overcome with clarity and a lack of baggage. Any parent who has made it past adolescence will tell you that the teen years are excruciatingly challenging. At that stage, young people begin to develop their ideas and experience life for themselves. No longer can we shield them from certain truths and realities nor can we diminish their impact upon them. Therefore, when a child is experiencing a difficult time brought on by a bad choice or the family dynamics, as mothers, we can tend to think like Hagar that there is nothing we can do.

In the middle of the pain and agony that Ismael and Hagar were going through brought on by their physical needs and heartbreak over the dissolution of their family, God intervened by sending an angel. The Lord's messenger approached the distraught mother with concern and tenderness and asked her what was the cause of her distress. As she stood in front of the angel, Hagar may have felt pangs of guilt and shame. She was a woman that could easily be viewed as receiving what she deserved. Her actions leading up to the moment she was ousted were less than exemplary; she was described, during her pregnancy, as having hatred for Sarah and was complicit in the toxic relationship they shared. In addition, we could even heap upon her Ishmael's bullying, which provided the excuse to have them sent away from the camp.

Today, like Hagar, we have our own set of items that occurred in the past which could give us cause to feel uncomfortable and guilt-ridden in the presence of God. A single mother that was never married can experience the term "single mother" as a veritable scarlet letter, a reminder that things were not done in the right order. A woman who has gone through a divorce could also feel that she should have tried harder to keep the family together.

What's interesting is that when the angel addressed Hagar, there were no words of condemnation or rehash of the past. Instead, he made sure to mention that God had heard the distress of the boy and then went into action to alleviate the situation. If she had nurtured any thoughts that her child was born under the wrong circumstances, the angel's actions would have contradicted them. Ishmael, as we know, was not the child of promise, as God hadn't ordained the union between Abraham and Hagar, yet the angel stated that God heard the cry of the boy. Ishmael's cry wasn't simply for lack of water but of anguish at the loss of relationship with his father and home. It couldn't be any clearer that the Lord was not going to let a child perish due to the actions of his parents.

The brief interchange between the angel and Hagar demonstrates that the Lord isn't going to allow a barrier consisting of a record of wrongs and what should have been between Him and us. Our actions, misplaced perceptions about being a single mother, or thoughts about the legitimacy of our children in no way restrains Him from being gracious, merciful, and compassionate. Based on Hagar's example, He seems much more concerned with the child's well-being and pointing the mother toward a vision of the future. In doing so, He would not keep her tethered to the past. A clear head and a light load was needed to help the child arrive at his destination. It's imperative that as single mothers, we take a look at this aspect of Hagar's life and realize God's ultimate objective. The Lord's example was one of moving forward and outlining what lay ahead. He spent no time discussing the validity of the bad breakup, the father who walked away, or how terrible things were at the moment. Whatever happened earlier was left in the past as He was pointing her forward toward the second portion of her journey.

Child Support

To think that a single mother who lived more than two thousand years ago could have anything to contribute toward the issue of child support is truly amazing, yet Hagar's story, in effect, gives us a model to deal with this very issue. As she and the boy were being put out of the family compound in the first part of Genesis 21:14, the Bible indicates that a backpack was placed on her shoulders containing some bread and water. Aside from the two items, no further indication is given as to any additional resources that may have been handed to her. I can't imagine that even in ancient times the meager rations she received would have adequately sustained her son through a few days, months, or even years of his life. How was this mother supposed to provide and care for her child with such a pittance?

More than two thousand years later, it's remarkable, but modern-day single mothers remain the recipients of nonexistent or insufficient child support in sums that can't adequately assist in pro-

viding for a child's needs such as housing, educa-
tion, clothing, and proper feeding. Many of us
have either experienced or have had discussions
with other single mothers concerning the challenges of caring for our children and meeting
household obligations while maintaining full-time
employment. The pressure of providing it all and
being it all can put tremendous strain on the
shoulders of a single mother. As Hagar gets further into her journey, her experiences seem to bear
witness to this very fact.

When Hagar departed from the camp, all of
the responsibilities of provider, protector, and
leader were deposited on her shoulders along with
the satchel of bread and water. Soon after she left,
she became overwhelmed by having to fulfill all of
her new roles simultaneously. Her son's emotional
breakdown necessitated a caretaker, his need for
water required a provider of resources. At the
same time he also needed someone with a clear
head to lead him past the unpleasantness of the
moment and toward the future. Hagar was inca-
pable of managing all of her child's needs, realiz-
ing how impossible her tasks seemed she cried out

in distress and crumbled just a few yards from her son.

Thankfully, God arrived in the form of an angel and pointed the mother to the physical resource that her child so desperately needed. Having read the account a number of times and in various translations, I found out that there was no indication that the Lord magically made the well appear. The implication seems to be that the well of water was already there. Overwhelmed by the weight of her emotions, Hagar was unable to see the opportunity that was within her reach. When she cried out to the Lord, it had to be a cry for help and an acknowledgment of her limitations. Once the Lord arrived, she had a partner, and the burden of doing it all alone was alleviated. With His help, she'd be able to see more clearly.

This portion of Hagar's story demonstrates that in instances when we are overcome by worry because the child support has not arrived or the sum is too small, crying out to the Lord is the first step in achieving a solution. He is the consummate provider. In each single mother's life, He will manifest provision and will do so in a unique manner for each woman. For some, it may be the miraculous appearance of resources, and for another, He may open their eyes to opportunities that they would not normally notice or gain without His direction. Turning to Him as a provider will ensure that our children will not suffer lack.

If He did it for Hagar, we can rest assured that He will do it for us. Our Lord does not play favorites. As added support to our belief that God will provide for us we can even turn to Philippians 4:19, which expressly invites us to trust in His provision. Notice that this passage is clear on who the source is and the limitless resources that God has at his disposal. We have nothing to do with the equation except the act of trusting Him, all or our needs and that of our children can be met by our great and awesome God.

And my God will meet all your needs according to the riches of his glory in Christ Jesus. (Philippians 4:19 NIV)

Lift them up

When the angel came to Hagar and spoke to her, he directed her to lift up the boy. In light of what was happening, this gesture seems obvious. After all, it can be said that this is a clear action that was necessary to comfort the distressed child and would also help him in receiving the water that he desperately needed. Peering below the surface, since we know that the stories in the Bible are given to us as models, we can view his prompting to the mother to lift up Ishmael as a call to prayer.

When the angel arrived, he could have immediately begun to take control of the situation and act on God's behalf. Instead, he invited the mother to express her burden and speak what was on her heart. A look at the definition of prayer reveals the same thing, according to the Oxford dictionary a prayer is a solemn request for help. Staring at the potential death of her child, when she spoke to the angel it had to have been about her concern for the well being of her child. Her words were in essence a solemn request for help, she was lifting him up in prayer both physically and figuratively.

On the journey to adulthood, our children will undoubtedly go through difficult stages and as they age our influence will diminish. During these instances, we may think that we're powerless to help and believe that our only option is to sit far off and watch helplessly, but our communication with the Lord, and our lifting them up is what will see them through every circumstance. Hagar believed her child's future was at risk, and she felt powerless to change what seemed to be an irreversible end. Divine assistance was essential and therefore she was prompted to lift him up and watch the change that would occur when the Lord intervened.

It's important to understand that prayer isn't something out of the ordinary but a simple conversation where we are vocal with the Lord about what is troubling us. With God, there is never a moment where a situation can't be reversed or made better, but to do so, it requires us to speak to Him. I'm reminded of the scripture in Hebrews

4:16 where we are urged to approach God's throne of grace where we will find help in times of need. Though that scripture applies to all of God's children, as single mothers, Hagar's story brings it closer to home. We are more apt to believe that the Lord hears our pleas, helps and provides mercy when we see it in the life of someone like us.

> Let's therefore draw near with boldness to the throne of grace, that we may receive mercy and may find grace for help in time of need.(Hebrews 4:16 WEB)

Hope and a future

One of the greatest concerns in the life of a single mother is the future of her offspring. In Hagar's case, as she assessed the external circumstances, which included a lack of resources, a child besieged by grief, and a road unclearly defined, she was inclined to believe that his future held no promise. This realization caused her despair, her vision was clouded, and she couldn't progress forward. Today, single moms face similar circumstances in the form of statistical forecasts that pronounce bleak and unsuccessful futures for children from single parent households. Often the knowledge of these statistics can foster anxiety and seek to rob the family of hope, which is one of the essential ingredients of life.

In Ishmael's example, once his mother lifted him up toward the Lord, God then began to tackle his future. The angel announced that God would make a great nation of Ishmael. The usage of the word "great" in describing Ishmael's future is of no inconsequential meaning. Today, the word is often used indiscriminately—we can have a great day or watch a great movie. It's used so frequently that we've lost the real impact of what the word means. According to Merriam-Webster's dictionary, you will find the definition of "great" includes eminent, distinguished, remarkably skilled, markedly superior in character or quality, and chief or prominent over others. A life of success and prominence was the future the Lord had prepared for the child of this single mother.

Words such as "distinguished," "remarkably skilled," and "markedly superior in quality" are not often utilized in describing the futures of children from single parent households. Instead, political pundits and the media flood us with negative statistics that declare doomed futures for children raised in single parent households. Hope and a vision of the future is life sustaining as echoed in Proverbs 29:18: "Where there is no vision, the people perish." Therefore, a statistic that asserts a child will grow up to be less than another because he or she is from a single parent household attempts to deny this child of his or her God-given hope. A school, or an instructor, that expects less from a child because he or she has only one parent at home does the same thing. A mother who succumbs to stress and berates a child by saying that he or she will never amount to anything robs the child of one the greatest gifts God has provided for us all in Jeremiah 29:11.

"For I know the plans I have for you" declares the Lord "plans to prosper you and not to harm you, plans to give you hope and a future."(Jeremiah 29:11 NIV)

Ishmael is a testament to the fact that we don't have to believe statistics and negative chatter about children from single parent households. It doesn't mean that because a child came from a single parent home, he or she will repeat the mistakes of his or her parents. A child whose mother was unwed has the same possibility as anyone else to enjoy a married relationship when they become of age.

Ishmael, the product of a single parent household, seemed to have enjoyed a fulfilling life as recorded in Genesis 21:20-21. Here we learn that he became an expert in his field, got married, and raised a family. More importantly, it's said that the Lord was with him throughout his life. As single moms, we have to look at God's Word for a vision of our children's future because it is up to Him to determine who and what they will be. Ultimately, it is our responsibility to lift them to the Lord in prayer daily, asking Him to guide them into the lives that He has set out for them.

The Widow in Zarephath

The Cultivation of Great Faith

The widow in Zarephath is another single mother easily missed not only due to her proximity to the great prophet Elijah but also because she is referred to as a widow. A woman whose marriage has fallen apart or a single woman never married wouldn't immediately identify with her as a single mother. It isn't until we take a look at the realities of her life that we realize that she is indeed a single mother with all of the responsibility to provide, raise, and care for her child alone. If we can see her in this context, she becomes relatable, and her story can provide some insight on how to live the single mom life during difficult times such as economic uncertainty, a faith crisis, questioning the tithe, worry for our children's future, and coping with the weight of sin and guilt.

The account of the widow is found in 1 Kings 17:7-24. She was living during the time of King Ahab, the ruler of Northern Israel. A man considered the worst king to have ever ruled Israel, he was married to a foreign princess named Jezebel, and the two wreaked havoc on the nation. They made a formidable duo, permitting nothing and no one to get in the way of their goals. They had no fear or regard for Yahweh—the God of Israel—and instituted across the land the worship of the fertility god, Baal. Their new god demanded forms of worship which included human sacrifice, self-flagellation, ritualistic prostitution, and child sacrifice. These practices were alien to the people of Israel at that time. As a servant of God, Elijah became angered at the direction in which the new rulers were taking the country; he, therefore, decided to take action against the monarchy.

One day, Elijah stood in the public square and proclaimed that it would no longer rain across the land until he declared otherwise. This pronouncement was not only a challenge to the king and queen's power but also a direct attack on the potency of the god Baal since he was attributed with making it rain. After this bold move, Elijah departed the city since God instructed him to leave the region and hide somewhere else.

> Then the word of the Lord came to Elijah: "Leave here, turn eastward and hide in the Kerith Ravine, east of the Jordan. You will drink from the brook, and I have directed the ravens to supply you with food there." (1 Kings 17:2-4 NIV)

As intended, the lack of rain over the next few years caused a severe drought. In this primarily agrarian society dependent on crops and livestock, the drought caused a great havoc on the economy. The animals began to die from dehydration, crops failed, and all across the nation people began to suffer. The brook where the Lord had sent Elijah to be cared for by birds eventually ran dry. God had to reposition the prophet to another location, and He sent him to another unlikely caretaker, that being a single mother living in Zarephath (1 Kings 17:8-17).

> Then the word of the LORD came to him: "Go at once to Zarephath in the region of Sidon and stay there. I have commanded a widow in that place to supply you with food." (1 Kings 17:8-9 NIV)

After spending weeks alone by the brook with no one to speak to and living on the morsels of food brought to him by the scavenger birds, Elijah was most likely relieved at the thought of access to a comfortable bed to sleep in, warm food to eat, and the company of other human beings.

> So he arose and went to Zarephath; and when he came to the gate of the city, behold, a widow was there gathering sticks.... (1 Kings 17:10 WEB)

When Elijah arrived in Zarephath, he met not just any widow gathering sticks by the main gates but the woman that God had told him about.

Could this be a coincidence that they met each other at the gate at that exact moment or an example of a divine appointment? On the surface, it may seem like a minute detail, one that doesn't need mentioning, but in fact, it forms the basis of an important lesson—that of a divine appointment.

A divine appointment is a union arranged by God for the purpose of carrying out His will. He may send someone to impart a word of wisdom that He whispered to us in private, and as such, the person is simply providing us with some heavenly confirmation. In other instances, He may send someone to open a door in the form of a lead or an opportunity. The Lord is always looking to use His servants as His hands and feet to bless someone, whether it be in the form of paying a bill or someones rent, buying groceries, etc. The situations are as varied as the individuals and His purposes.

One of the greatest threats to the Christian life is losing sight of God and forgetting that He is active and involved in our lives. The concept of

47

divine appointment serves a two-fold purpose: it helps us to see the Lord working, and more importantly, it reminds us that we are potential partners with Him once we submit to His prompting. In the story of the single mother of Zarephath, she enjoyed a double blessing; she was the Lord's helper as the 'caregiver' to the prophet, and she was also blessed with a lesson in faith.

As the story goes, Elijah, in accordance to what God revealed to him, engaged the woman as one who had a duty toward him by asking for water and food.

> He called to her and said, "Please get me a little water in a jar, that I may have a drink." As she was going to get it, he called, " Please bring me a morsel of bread in your hand." (1 Kings 17:10-11 WEB)

Upon hearing his request for water, she quickly abandoned her task and began to walk toward the town well to draw him some water. No sooner had she taken a few steps than she heard Elijah asking her to bring him some food. It was just that

morning that she'd reassessed the contents of her
pantry, and nothing had changed except that there
was less today than yesterday, not even enough to
make a full meal to feed herself and her son. As
hospitable as she'd wanted to be, there was no way
she could honor his last request. Perhaps shame
and hopelessness caused her to blurt out the truth
of her desperate situation. She had to tell him that
she couldn't accommodate him; there simply
wasn't enough.

> "As surely as the LORD your God lives,"
> she replied, "I don't have any bread—only
> a handful of flour in a jar and a little oil in
> a jug. I am gathering a few sticks to take
> home and make a meal for myself and my
> son, that we may eat it—and die." (1 Kings
> 17:12 NIV)

You will remember verse 9 explicitly states
that God had spoken to her. Why wasn't she will-
ing to part with some of the food as well? Could it
be that she had simply gone deaf to His voice because she was allowing the state of her present
circumstances to speak to her mind? Perhaps dur-

ing a more robust economy, she would have generously offered Elijah a place at her table, but now that there wasn't enough for a full meal for herself and her precious son, she had to think of her family first.

I can imagine that life for her was going well before the economy went down; she had a steady means of supporting herself and thinking that she had only herself to rely on must have prompted her to be a good budgeter. The fact that she had enough resources to last her weeks into the drought was a testament to her exceptional management skills. Without any fault of her own, life took an unexpected turn; as the drought intensified and the economy tanked, she was no longer able to provide for herself and her child. The money ran out and her resources began to dwindle. She no doubt prayed for the Lord to intervene, but nothing happened. Eventually, when God didn't show up, doubt began to creep in. Was He too busy, or was she being punished for a past sin? Was God even real? Was it worth it to live a righteous life? Slowly, anxiety and fear began to set in; she decided to turn to the social and economic climate for cues on how to live.

> Elijah said to her, "Don't be afraid. . . ."
> (1 Kings 17:13 NIV)

Her voice revealed her anxiety because the prophet picked up on it and gently admonished her not to be afraid. She didn't know this, but God had answered her prayers and sent to her door a brother in the faith—a person with a testimony—who would point her back toward a relationship and trust in the Lord. The stranger with whom she was speaking had recently been in a precarious situation, of which it was no easy feat for him to stand alone against the reigning king and queen of the land. A change in circumstances wasn't instantaneous; God didn't zap King Ahab and Queen Jezebel off the throne or evaporate every drop of water in the land at once. Instead, the corrupt rulers were still in power, and they were out to capture the prophet who prophesied "doom" on the land. Of course, Elijah suffered through the effect of the drought along with everyone else, though he received his sustenance from little birds. Elijah had to put all of his trust in the Lord and rely on God's timing rather than give weight to what was occurring around him.

The Lord had sent the prophet to shake His daughter and remove the fear out of her life. He knew the danger of allowing her to continue to nurture that negative emotion and the detriment it was having on her life and potentially on that of her child. Fear, doubt, and hopelessness had made her susceptible to voices other than God's. Elijah's presence would help to reignite this single mom's faith in the Lord, which in turn would allow her to tap into the abundant blessings that He had in store for her. Elijah, therefore, repeated his request for food but added that she must not only share her food with him but serve him first.

> " . .go home and do as you have said. But first make a small cake of bread for me from what you have and bring it to me, and then make something for yourself and your son. For this is what the LORD, the God of Israel, says: 'The jar of flour will not be used up, and the jug of oil will not run dry until the day the

LORD gives rain on the land." (1 Kings 17:13-14 NIV)

In making that statement, he was inspiring her to put into practice Hebrews 11:1.

Now faith is assurance of things hoped for, proof of things not seen. (Hebrews 11:1 WEB)

What she hoped for was a secure future for her child and food for them to eat, but right in front of her was a hungry man with dirty clothes. There was no way to know with absolute certainty that this man was telling the truth because during the time in which she lived, a woman alone in any part of the city was especially at risk to scoundrels and scammers. What if this man had run out of food and merely tried to trick her into parting with her last meal? Albeit dirty and unkempt, there was something about him, something that spoke to her heart and brought back the words that the Lord had spoken to her. There was no outward sign that she would not run out of food once she cared for him, she pushed past fear and doubt and chose to put her faith into action.

> She went away and did as Elijah had
> told her. So there was food every day for
> Elijah and the woman and her family.
> For the jar of flour was not used up and
> the jug of oil did not run dry, in keeping
> with the word of the LORD spoken by
> Elijah. (1 Kings 17:15-16 NIV)

As she walked home, every step must have been agonizing because once fear and doubt set in, it's not easy to be rid of them. Add to that the instinct of self-preservation, the walk home must have been difficult. The voices in her head must have screamed and told her to stop; they must have told her that there was no guarantee, and she should certainly not give to someone else first before taking care of her child or herself. We notice that she made the choice to listen to God and went home to prepare the meal.

The widow chose to follow God and, true to His word, for the duration of the drought both she and her family were provided for. The Lord's abundance didn't depend on the economy; while the entire country was facing economic upheaval, she and her family were blessed beyond measure throughout the drought. It can also be said that not just her son and Elijah were recipients of her obedience. It's mentioned that her family were also partakers. The addition of the words "her family" points to the possibility that her extended family were also present. In those days, families lived in close quarters, so it is possible that her parents or even brothers and sisters enjoyed full bellies during the drought.

Hearing Voices

In the story, it was mentioned that God had spoken to the widow, but as we read, she really isn't behaving at first as if she had actually heard God's voice. This portion of the story had me thinking about this notion of hearing voices, though not as it relates to schizophrenia but the fact that we live in a time where our lives are filled with voices. The media isn't only restricted to the television in the living room or the radio in the car. We are now followed at the gas pump, grocery counter, work desktop, back seat cabin of a taxi, airplane, and the list grows daily as marketers devise methods to reach us.

With all of this noise, the Lord is also trying to speak to us and does so on a regular basis during our quiet devotional time, through church sermons, Bible studies, divine appointments, a persistent, still, small voice, or a strong desire in your heart that is aligned with His word. Often the prompting to start a new business, go to school, write, serve on a ministry, extend yourself to another, or any of the myriads of things that are pulling at the strings of your heart may very well be the Lord calling you for His use. He may have need of your talents, abilities, or resources— abundant or limited.

The call may not occur under ideal circumstances. It may happen during times when you have suffered loss or barely have enough. Often, like the widow, when we peer into our proverbial cupboards, we may see what is missing and reason that since we don't have a husband, more time, lots of money, super intelligence, or connections to the right people, then it was a mistake, and God didn't speak. Sometimes our well-meaning friends and family, who would not want us to suffer harm, can also deter us from what the Lord has told us to do, advising us instead that as single mothers we should always think of securing our resources and leading safe and careful lives. Let's not forget the 24-hour news cycle intent on informing us of the "realities" of life from the dismal unemployment rate and single parent statistics to the latest tragedy or foreign threat. Whether we realize it or not, these voices are often the ones influencing us as we make decisions rather than staying focused on what God's is telling us to do.

The widow's story brings out a few scriptures that we can use whenever we are facing a tough decision or when we need to question the Lord's voice.

Trust in the Lord with all your heart, And lean not on your own understanding; In all your ways submit to him,And

57

he will make your paths straight.
(Proverbs 3:5-6 NIV)

It bears repeating that the widow relied on her understanding; there was no way that she could take care of Elijah with her limited means. With this in mind, it's important to realize that as Christians, there are two realities: the one we think we see with our limited, finite sight and that of the Lord, who surveys the past, the present, and the future. When we solely rely on social and economic indicators to inform us, we are relying on our own understanding and cannot tap into the limitless blessings that God has available. If God has whispered something that you can't see happening, just obey. He will take care of the details.

"My sheep hear my voice, and I know them, and they follow me." (John 10:27 WEB)

The best way to remain attuned to Him is through constant interaction, which means a consistent and steady prayer life. How do we do this when our lives are busy with the demands of our time resembling that of a superhero's schedule? There is no easy answer or way around it; we simply have to make Him a priority before our day even gets started.

"Call to me, and I will answer you, and will show you great and difficult things, which you don't know." (Jeremiah 33:3 WEB)

In keeping with the idea that we need to be in constant communication with the Lord, we have to communicate our needs and struggles with Him. Though He knows our needs already, the Lord is someone who desires relationship. He wants us to get into a dialogue with Him and tell Him our challenges. In the story of the widow, Elijah as a stand-in for God, commanded her to do something that she thought was impossible. She, in desperation, opened up to him and let him know what she believed to be the impossibility of carrying out his wishes. Once she spoke to him and revealed her thoughts, he was then able to share with her what she did not know. Elijah didn't go into the mechanics of how the Lord would provide. He just said that He would. So when we are facing a challenge, we just need to speak to Him and trust in his instructions.

"Seek the Kingdom of God above all else, and live righteously, and he will give you everything you need." (Matthew 6:33 NLT)

Once we have made Him a priority and stay in contact with Him, we are showing the Lord that we are more interested in His kingdom and then our agendas. When the Lord is the focus, it's incredible how everything else falls into place, and once the widow took her eyes off of her need and what was going on around her, the Lord gave her all that she needed.

The Need for Wise Counsel

Earlier I discussed the trouble that the widow had in hearing God speak to her. She must have recognized Elijah as the person the Lord had asked her to care for, but in the midst of the economic upheaval and her personal distress, she was about to walk away from God's command and the potential blessing that was to come. The widow is not unique in this situation because it's very easy to follow God's voice when everything is going well, but when things are shaky or uncertain, we can easily fool ourselves into thinking that we misheard Him. Moreover, just as the widow showed her eagerness to get the water and comply with just a portion of what the Lord commanded, we too may want to fool ourselves into thinking that we are following God. Admittedly, obeying God's voice in the midst of troubled times can be a challenge, and when we are confused as to whether we heard properly, the Bible advises that we seek counsel.

> Where there is no counsel, the people fall; But in the multitude of counselors, there is safety. (Proverbs 11:14 NKJV)

In the midst of her crisis, Elijah served as the wise counsel. He understood that carrying out the Lord's objectives would ultimately stretch her toward a higher plane where she would experience a deeper relationship with God. As a wise brother in the faith, Elijah didn't make things easy for her or accept her excuses. As a good counselor, he advised her to push past her fears. He challenged her to trigger her faith, listen to God's promptings, and do what seemed illogical. With Elijah's counsel, the widow was able to fulfill her divine purpose and, more importantly, experience the Lord in a tangible and real way.

Single moms like everyone face moments of crisis, and it's essential that we have a support system that includes wise counselors. As single mothers, we are particularly prone to isolation due to our busy schedules since much of our time is spent working, taking our children to events, going over homework, or executing household chores. There is often very little time to fellowship and develop healthy relationships with other Christians. However, when we are not connected, we can miss out on the advice of another in the faith who has an experience in the area we are facing. The single mom in Zarephath, in the midst of an impossible situation, needed to hear from a person who was trusting in God and walking in obedience.

The widow's story provides us with an example of the usefulness of keeping strong believers in our circle. Our fellow brothers and sisters in Christ can make a tremendous difference in our lives if they are grounded in a relationship with the Lord. It's important to mention, however, that we do not blindly bring people into our lives because they claim to be Christians; as the Bible states in 1 John 4:1, we must test the spirits to see if the way they live and counsel are aligned with the word of God.

> Dear friends, do not believe everyone who claims to speak by the Spirit. You must test them to see if the spirit they have comes from God. For there are many false prophets in the world. (1 John 4:1 NLT)

The Tithe and the Single Mom

As single mothers, we are acutely aware of how challenging the area of finances can be even when we are fortunate enough to receive consistent child support. Our incomes are often insufficient to satisfy the number of items needed for daily life such as the car loan, taxes, insurance (car, home, renters, and life), mortgage, rent, food, school fees, childcare, heating, cooling, electric, home, car repairs, etc. Lets not forget all of the additional expenses related to our children's needs and wants such as sports participation fees, tutoring to aid in academic achievement, vacations, the occasionally lost items such as the ninety dollar textbook, and a variety of elements that are as unique as our children. In many instances, we can find ourselves with a lot more month left than our finances can cover.

Tithing, as many of us have already experienced, can be a very difficult thing for us. Giving ten percent of your income when one hundred percent barely covers all of the expenses can often

64

tempt us to bypass the tithe. The widow, in fact, was in just such a quandary because not only were her resources inadequate but she was also in the midst an economic crash—a climate that is reminiscent of the recent crash of 2008.

At that time, people all across the nation were hurting. Many suffered job loss, had homes foreclosed, witnessed plummeting retirement accounts, and businesses vanished while the price of necessities such as food and gas increased. Stories circulated that even local pantries were running out of food. Single mothers were severely affected, and I was among them. The best financial gurus often speak of having a year's worth of surplus, but what would happen if the recession lasted more than one year? For those of us who were adversely affected by the crash of 2008 which continued into 2010, we were just like the widow staring into bare cupboards and wondering what would happen next and, more importantly, how were we going to give to the Lord when we simply didn't have enough.

In the widow's story and for those of us who

went through the recession, the key word is "enough." During the years of plenty, we were accustomed to a particular lifestyle and an abundance. When disaster struck, we weren't without; we simply had less. If you'll remember, the widow had something for the day. Her anxiousness and worry came in anticipation of tomorrow's needs and undoubtedly giving weight to the economic climate. The fact that God had spoken to her gives us an indication that she knew Him, but when trouble hit, she began to look at herself as the source, thus living contrary to the words in one of the Bible's most direct passages concerning God's provision - Mathew 6:25-33.

> "Therefore I tell you, do not be anxious about your life, what you will eat or what you will drink, nor about your body, what you will put on. Is not life more than food, and the body more than clothing? Look at the birds of the air: they neither sow nor reap nor gather into barns, and yet your heavenly Father feeds them. Are you not of more value than they?

Therefore do not be anxious, saying, 'What shall we eat?' or 'What shall we drink?' or 'What shall we wear?' your heavenly Father knows that you need them all. But seek first the kingdom of God and his righteousness, and all these things will be added to you." (Matthew 6:25-32 NIV)

The widow was literally, troubled about what she and her child would eat tomorrow.; On the surface this may seem like a simple question of food and groceries but in a broader context she was a single mother wrestling with the subject of tithing. When the prophet began to speak with her, he directly confronted her with an appeal not only to part with some of her resources but to dedicate a portion to him first. In the Bible God has made the same request, the passages in Proverbs 3:9 and Malachi 3:10 are identical to Elijah's approach with the widow

Honor the Lord with your wealthAnd with the firstfruits of all your produce; Then your barns will be filled with plenty, And your vats will be bursting with wine. (Proverbs 3:9-10 NIV)

67

"..Bring the whole tithe into the store-house, that there may be food in my house. Test me in this," says the Lord Almighty, "and see if I will not throw open the floodgates of heaven and pour out so much blessing that there will not be room enough to store it.." (Malachi 3:10 NIV)

Notice that there aren't any verses directly before or after Malachi and Proverbs that provide an exclusion for single mothers. In fact, the verses that prompt us to tithe follows the structure of the conversation that Elijah had with the widow. First, he makes the request and then follows up with a promise of blessing just at Proverbs 3:9-10. The second scripture invites us to test the Lord and His promises that we will not be blessed according to our ability but upon His riches and reputation.

It bears mentioning that this is not an invitation to fold our hands and do nothing nor does this give us license to live each day carefree by making poor decisions because we know that God will provide. The tithe is by no means a salvation issue; no one is going to hell for not tithing. The tithe is simply a vehicle that demonstrates our trust in the Lord and allows for a practical perspective on materialism. When we tithe, we put into practice Philippians 4:19, and allow God to demonstrate His participation in our lives.

> And my God shall supply all your need according to His riches and glory by Christ (Philippians 4:19 NKJV)

The tithe is a general call that God makes to us all, but when we read about a single mom with limited means being challenged to comply we modern single mothers should stop and take notice. What's more, the woman experienced difficulty during an economic upheaval that affected the entire nation. As unpredictable as life is, we know that even during times of plenty we can personally undergo moments of financial strain. The story of this single mother in Zarephath is there to remind us that God is very aware of our needs and always arrives just in time. We should therefore never become tightfisted or bypass the tithe because we are concerned about the economic climate. As demonstrated in this story the Lord is not constrained by economic indicators, we have to remember that it all belongs to him anyway.

> To the LORD your God belong the heavens, even the highest heavens, the earth and everything in it. (Deuteronomy 10:14 NIV)

> For all the world is mine and everything in it.(Psalm 50:12 NLT)

> "The silver is mine and the gold is mine," declares the LORD Almighty. (Haggai 2:8 NIV)

> For every beast of the forest is mine, and the cattle on a thousand hills. (Psalm 50:10 NKJV)

Since God owns it all, he is the ultimate source and has a solution to all of our fiscal problems. Our job is to learn from the single mom in Zarephath, incline our ears toward God, surrender to Him what little we have and exercise our faith by following His commands.

The Weight of Guilt

The story of the widow of Zarephath didn't just end with a demonstration of provision and a happily ever after; her story continues with a very somber event.

> Some time later the son of the woman who owned the house became ill. He grew worse and worse and finally stopped breathing. She said to Elijah, "What do you have against me, man of God? Did you come to remind me of my sin and kill my son?"
>
> "Give me your son," Elijah replied. He took him from her arms, carried him to the upper room where he was staying, and laid him on his bed. Then he cried

out to the LORD, "O LORD my God, have you brought tragedy also upon this widow I am staying with, by causing her son to die?"

Then he stretched himself out on the boy three times and cried to the LORD, "O LORD my God, let this boy's life return to him!" The LORD heard Elijah's cry, and the boy's life returned to him, and he lived. Elijah picked up the child and carried him down from the room into the house. He gave him to his mother and said, "Look, your son is alive!"

Then the woman said to Elijah, "Now I know that you are a man of God and that the word of the LORD from your mouth is the truth." (1 Kings 17:17-24 NLT)

After the amazing high of witnessing a personal, tangible manifestation of the Lord's hand, the widow suffers a major blow. Her only son became ill and soon died. In reading her reaction, she hardly seemed to be a woman who had learned to trust in God, but then again, how calm and rational would any of us be if our child suddenly passed away? Interestingly, she seems to be blaming a past sin for her son's death. "Did you come to remind me of my sin?" she asks the prophet. Apparently, something had occurred in her life that made her believe God was holding it against her. During the entire time she had received His blessing, it seemed there was a part of her that was waiting for the proverbial other shoe to drop, and so it did.

While she'd experienced God's goodness and mercy, there was a part of her that was holding on to a past sin, making it impossible to fully enjoy and surrender to the Lord. The widow is not alone in harboring these types of feelings. Many of us can carry the burden of guilt from a past sin and refuse to let it go because we feel we are unworthy of the love and care that God has to offer. When anything goes wrong, we most often think that God is punishing us or settling an old score.

The Lord was not looking to punish the widow, nor is He out to get us when He allows painful events in our lives, Psalm 103:12 gives us insight into God's heart as it relates to forgiveness of sins. God's greatest goal is a sincere and authentic relationship with us. He sees deep into our souls and knows our challenges and what areas need to be improved. He wasn't finished with the widow when He made the miracle of provision. There was still more work to do; He wanted this woman to understand intimately and completely who He was. Moreover, His aim was to liberate her from any obstacle that was limiting their relationship.

As far as the east is from the west, so far has he removed our transgressions from us. (Psalm 103:12 NIV)

Through the prophet Elijah, the Lord brought her son back to life. While not expressly mentioned in the story at no time did the prophet ask her what her past sin was nor did the Lord give any indication that He was punishing her for the past. As her child was returned to her, she seemed to have arrived at a point that she knew and could recognize the Lord as evidenced by her exclamation to Elijah: "Now I know that you are a man of God and that the word of the LORD from your mouth is the truth." When she began her journey, she was unsure if she had even heard God's voice. At the end she is able to discern truth and most importantly the voice of the Lord.

Gods aim in this single mothers life was to bring her to a place where she could distinguish his voice and trust him. His desire for the single mother of today has not changed. The Lord wants us to entrust him with our lives, worries, resources and children. In one word He just wants us to trust Him.

The Widow With The Oil

Debt Free Entrepreneur

Each interaction God has had with the single mothers in the Bible has specific echoes to situations and issues that we face today. In the very short passage found in 2 Kings 4:1-7 below, we will read about a single mother who transitioned from a desperately indebted woman caring for two boys at risk to a debt-free entrepreneur and role model.

One day, the widow of a member of the

group of prophets came to Elisha and cried out, "My husband who served you is dead, and you know how he feared the Lord. But now a creditor has come, threatening to take my two sons as slaves."

"What can I do to help you?" Elisha asked. "Tell me, what do you have in the house?"

"Nothing at all, except a flask of olive oil," she replied.

And Elisha said, "Borrow as many empty jars as you can from your friends and neighbors. Then go into your house with your sons and shut the door behind you. Pour olive oil from your flask into the jars, setting each one aside when it is filled."

So she did as she was told. Her sons kept bringing jars to her, and she filled one after another. Soon every container was full to the brim!

"Bring me another jar," she said to one of her sons. "There aren't anymore!" he told her. And then the olive oil stopped flowing.

When she told the man of God what had happened, he said to her, "Now sell the olive oil and pay your debts, and you and your sons can live on what is left over." (2 Kings 4:1-7 NLT)

Having read the passage above, you have no doubt noticed that this woman was in dire straits. Her husband had just died and left her with an insurmountable amount of debt. During the time she lived, it was a common practice that if a person was unable to pay their debts, they were to submit themselves to their creditors and labor for six years to pay off the money owed. What's more, the threat of slavery was not just reserved for the debtor but extended to the entire family as well. This single mother was in just such a crisis. One of her creditors had expressed his right to take her two boys as laborers to pay what must have been a sizable debt. In despair, she turned to God through the prophet Elisha.

As far as we can tell from the reading, the widow did nothing wrong; she was just affected by an unforeseen occurrence. Today, we too can suffer an unexpected event that can land us in debt, such as medical bills from an illness, a job layoff, car repair, house maintenance cost, and much more. Other times, it can be a flirtation with credit cards, with the intention that they will be paid off quickly, but then things get out of control, and before long, we are in hot water with the credit card company.

Thankfully, we are no longer subject to having our children whisked away to pay our debts, but we can indeed live under the threat of home foreclosure, automobile repossession, or incessant calls from creditors. Once in debt, a poor credit rating can put limits on our lives by prohibiting us from gaining a better paying job, bring us face-to-face with an undue increase in insurance rates, as well as keep us from purchasing a new home. A single mom in debt is often a woman at the mercy of creditors much like the widow.

God did not create His children to live a life of bondage, especially that of debt. Romans 13:8 states that we should "owe no one anything, except to love each other." Proverbs 22:7 also forewarns us about the condition of a debtor by saying "the borrower is a servant to the lender." In Mathew 6:24, it's stated, "No one can serve two masters. Either he will hate the one and love the other, or he will be devoted to the one and despise the other. You cannot serve both God and money." Though this last verse is often used to refer to someone who idolizes money, it can also describe a person who has become preoccupied with his or her financial obligations.

When debt collectors are calling, the mailbox is flooded with past due notices, and most of the day is spent consumed by worrying about the bills and the amount owed, we have in essence become a servant to money. No longer is money a vehicle for the advancement of God's work but it becomes a horrible task master that robs us of peace, joy, and the fulfillment of our potential.

What do you have ?

Once the prophet heard the mother's plea, he asked what he could do about her situation. He then followed up with the question, "What do you have?" In asking what she had, Elisha employed a principle that God has repeatedly used throughout Scripture when someone was contending with worry, anxiety, or when someone was unsure of his or her capabilities. In Exodus 4:1-5, we see a perfect example of God's use of this principle. If you are not familiar with the account, the following is a very brief recap.

At a riverside, Moses as a baby was found by the daughter of the great Pharaoh; although a Hebrew, he was raised as an Egyptian prince. Many years later, Moses discovered his identity and was angered when he saw an Egyptian abusing a Hebrew slave. Overcome by rage, he murdered the man and soon after went into exile. Moses spent the next forty years in the desert, away from the prestige of the palace courts.

One day, while tending his animals, Moses had

an encounter with God on a mountain top in the presence of a burning bush. At the time, the Lord revealed to Moses the assignment he was created for: he was the ordained liberator of the children of Israel. Years of hard labor and a nomadic life had erased the identity of an Egyptian prince and what now stood before God was a humble shepherd. The Lord commanded Moses to return to his old life not as the heir to the throne of Pharaoh but as the shepherd he had become. Doubtful he'd be of any use to the Lord's plan, Moses exposes his insecurities and fears that no one would listen to him. Once Moses verbalized his concerns, the Lord questioned him by asking, "What is that in your hand?" Exodus 4:2. At the time, all Moses could offer God was his shepherd's staff, an item that helped to nudge his livestock in line and often served as a walking aid. Once Moses submitted his staff to God, the simple stick became a mighty instrument of power that would part the Red Sea, transform into a serpent, and perform many other wondrous works.

Jesus utilized the same principle in Mathew 14:13-21 when challenged with feeding more than five thousand followers. After a long day of preaching to a multitude, they arrived in a desolate place where there were no vendors to sell food to the people. Worried, the apostles went to Jesus and implored Him to let the people go home. Undeterred, Jesus's reply was "What do you have?" All they had were five barley loaves and two pieces of fish; clearly this was inadequate to feed so many people. Jesus took that which was handed over to Him and multiplied it to feed more than five thousand men. The count is significantly more because Scripture states that the number of women and children were not counted. In both instances, once the concern and the minimal resources were submitted to God, He took responsibility for the magnification of was seemingly inconsequential.

The burdened single mom stood in front of God's prophet in much the same way that the apostles and Moses had in the face of what seemed to be an insurmountable hurdle. Available to the prophet was the possibility of asking other believers to help her by having them contribute to a collection designated for her family. Elisha could have also offered to use his influence as a religious leader to speak to the debtor on her behalf. He chose none of these options but instead asked this single mother to take stock of what she possessed. This tactic accomplished two things: first it took her mind off of the problem and made her think of what the Lord had given to her. Second there would be no denying the Lords activity in resolving her problem when she would consider her starting point and where she would end.

The widow had enough faith, which had led her to God's house for an answer but it was also necessary for her to move beyond a stance of prayer and supplication. Faith demands a physical demonstration of our beliefs much like the claims in Hebrews 11:1.

> Now faith is the substance of things hoped for, the evidence of things not seen. (Hebrews 11:1NIV)

She had never seen anyone before herself bailed out of trouble through the collection of empty oil jars. She operated entirely out of faith in the living God. The Lord had given her the tools that would resolve her problem, but it would take action on her part combined with His presence to arrive at liberation. In such a small town everyone knew what was going on with her, they were no doubt curious as they saw her walk to and from various neighbors' homes asking for empty vessels.

If she felt any sense of shame or discomfort, she had to move beyond that only keeping in mind the vision of a secure future for her boys. She remained focused and heeded the prophet's words of not only collecting just enough jars but exhausting every opportunity and trusting God to go above and beyond her expectations. The widow carried on, and finally, after she had asked the very last person for an empty jar, she went home and closed the door as the prophet had instructed.

In today's society, we are almost always preoccupied with managing our day to day obligations. When we add debt to the equation, it makes for a stressful and often desperate existence. In a state of stress or desperation, it's nearly impossible to assess the gifts and tools that God has already given us. In the account of the widow with the oil, we get to see firsthand how the Lord wants us to respond to what on the surface seems to be an impossible situation. Our first step should always be to turn to God, He will give us an answer. To resolve our problem in the best way possible we need a word from God. Quick five minute prayers and then creating our own solutions will never result in receiving Gods best. The Bible tells us in Jeremiah 33:3, that when we are at a loss and need clarification God promises to communicate with us.

"Call to Me, and I will answer you, and show you great and mighty things, which you do not know." (Jeremiah 33:3 NKJV)

Once we've made our petition to God and listened carefully for his direction, it's important to take our eyes off of the problem and take stock of the resources that we are underutilizing. All of us have been gifted with something, whether it be a fantastic singing voice, culinary aptitude, business acumen, a life-changing product, writing ability, radio show talent, sewing skills, a blogging concept, or any of the myriad of items stored within us or found in our homes. Much like the widow, Moses, and the apostles, these are the tools that we have in our hands that God can magnify to solve our challenges and help us construct more satisfying lives.

Debt Free Entrepreneur

No matter how things seem, there is always Gods perspective. The Lords plan for us is always more than we ever hope or imagine. When the prophet told the mother of two not to get "too few jars," he was prompting her into the next phase of life that God had prepared for her. Elisha speaking on behalf of God understood that in her stressful state, she wouldn't be thinking of a long-term plan. Her immediate need was to remove her children out of harms way. Therefore, she most likely would have only borrowed just enough to satisfy the debt. She probably never thought that God's generosity would extend to create a new way of life for her and her children. The extra jars of oil were to form the basis of a thriving family business.

In ancient times, oil was a very precious commodity because it was a time intensive substance to produce. Oil was utilized throughout all facets of life during that period; people needed oil not only for cooking but also to light their lamps in the evening; they used it for cosmetics, medicinal purposes, and even in the anointing of priests or kings. God didn't just pull her out of debt and leave it up to her to figure things out in the coming years; she received the ability to become resourceful and epitomize Jeremiah 29:11:

"For I know the plans I have for you," declares the LORD, "plans to prosper you and not to harm you, plans to give you hope and a future." (Jeremiah 21:11 NIV)

Imagine her surprise and delight as she took her small jar and filled the first container and then the next, and the one after that until all the jars had been filled. Could she have ever envisioned the magnitude of God's generosity? God had a plan for her as he does for all His children. He doesn't merely pull us out of one bad situation and watch us plummet into another. He wants to prosper us, and the concept of prospering isn't only related to our financial lives. The word prosper, means to blossom, progress, flourish physically as well as grow healthy and strong. With a new business, this family would indeed flourish, and the two young boys would be able to grow healthy and strong.

This type of blessing isn't reserved only for a woman who lived over two millennia ago; her challenges are easily recognizable today, for those of us single mothers, who dream of entrepreneurship but feel it's out of reach due to the weight of our responsibilities and financial obligations. This story is also relevant to a single mom who is being crushed under the burden of debt or a mother who is still reeling from the impact of the economic crisis of 2008. We all can be recipients of God's grace which affords us an opportunity to live out our dreams be it entrepreneurship or working for a company or profession that allow us to flourish. We need only remember the Widow with the Oil combined with the words of Ephesians 3:20.

> Now glory be to God, who by his mighty power at work within us is able to do far more than we would ever dare to ask or even dream of—infinitely beyond our highest prayers, desires, thoughts, or hopes. (Ephesians 3:20 TLB)

When Children are at risk

The stories of Hagar, The Widow of Zarephath and The Widow With the Oil all contain children at risk. Hagar's son almost died in the dessert, the Widow of Zarephath endured her child dying and being brought back to life and The Widow with the Oil was at risk of losing her children. It's no accident that in each of the accounts we looked at, the children have been in a situation where their future seemed uncertain. Though at the very outset, I criticized the media and their statistics which spoke of negative futures for children of single parent homes it's interesting to notice the Lord has tackled this subject through the stories we reviewed.

The reality is that children from single parent homes are prone to risk, it won't come from a creditor's threat to cart them off as chattel to satisfy a debt, but the notion of potential loss exists nonetheless. When mothers are working long hours and commuting great distances, it can be difficult for us to cultivate meaningful interactions with our children and be involved with every aspect of their day to day lives. In the absence of engaged and present parents, our children can be susceptible to others from households with opposing value systems, the media, chat room content, adults with malicious intent, gangs, or even drugs. Such outside factors can creep in and essentially cart them away to a life of bondage. What all of these stories have demonstrated however is that when we submit our children to the Lord, we allow Him to take responsibility for their future.

As mothers, it isn't merely enough to read Bible stories to our children and bring them to church. What becomes transformative is their ability to see God working and active in our lives when they are young. The widow with the oil gives us a component that we did not have before with the previous mothers. In addition to lifting them up in prayer, its essential for them to be active participants on our faith journey as the widow had. From going to see the prophet to knocking on each door in the neighborhood to retrieve the jars, these boys were able to experience the reality of a living God. The experience would forever transform these young men; it would serve as a basis for them to deepen their relationship with God. In the sight of such a miraculous occurrence, no longer would the Lord Yahweh be a concept taught by their mother, but at that moment, He was substantiated, and they experienced Psalm 46:1.

"God is our refuge and strength, a very present help in trouble."(Psalm 46:1NKJV)

These young men were aware that their future was in jeopardy, and the Lord came to help them.

He was their refuge from forfeiting critical years of their lives. God was indeed present. Regardless of what would happen in their future, they could always turn back to this experience and remember their mother's faith and God as provider and protector. Much like a work résumé outlying experiences accumulated over the years, it's paramount that our children develop a working knowledge of God and develop a résumé of experiences that begin in their youth.

> "Since my youth, O God you have taught me and to this day, I declare your marvelous deeds." (Psalm 71:17 NIV)

David's interactions with God as a youth formed the basis of his great faith and love of the Lord. As our children leave our homes, go to college, or enter the world, school professors, and their peers will challenge them regarding their Christian faith. It is the experiences of their youth with God that will see them through and outweigh the idle talk of naysayers, unbelievers, and negative influences.

A Role Model

More than ever in our modern society it seems as if someone is always watching what we do, especially with the proliferation of social media. The way we walk as single mothers can have a profound impact on other people. We are not only recipients of God's grace but also servants through whom He can make an impact in the lives of others. Our single mother status may sometimes make us prone to challenges in the financial arena, but we can use this as an awesome way to show off our Lord.

The Widow with the Oil had to have made quite an impact on the townspeople by living out her faith so publicly. Was it possible for her debt to be wiped out in another way? God could have moved the prophet to take up a collection on her behalf or even speak to the creditor as I mentioned before. He could have made the extra oil and vessels appear in her home out of thin air, but He didn't use any of these scenarios to assist her. She wasn't spared the humiliation of the creditor threatening to take her children, nor the walks through town with her boys in tow borrowing vessels. The Widow's problem and solution became a vehicle for the Lord to be glorified.

For days and weeks to come she would be an object of conversation. Neighbors, family, and friends would want to know what was the cause of her reversal from debt. In sharing her story, many people would have the opportunity to have their faith reignited or brought to the Lord. Let's not forget the unforgettable example she became not only on her two sons but on single mothers that have followed over these many hundreds of years.

One Last Lesson

The widow's story offers one more lesson. In the midst of life's challenges, we are often tempted to run to friends and confidants for prayer and advice. The widow chose to limit her conversation only to the man of God. It is wise, therefore, that we are careful in selecting the people with whom we share our dreams and difficulties. It's important to remember that everyone is at varying levels of faith. In the guise of being well-intentioned, we can be derailed from the plans that God has for our lives.

On the surface, it didn't seem feasible that a small jar of oil could be used as a solution to the massive mountain of debt that confronted her. If she had spoken to a practical friend, they may have dissuaded and advised that she should look at things realistically. Others may have come over and helped her to prepare for what would be the inevitable. No one could have imagined what God was going to do. However in 1 Corinthians 2:9 we are reminded that the Lord is a person who loves to surprise his children, our minds can not conceive what He is going to do from one moment to the next. The only thing we can be sure of is that it will always be a surprise. Had she confided in others she may have missed out on Gods grace.

But as it is written: "Eye has not seen, nor ear heard, Nor have entered into the heart

of man The things which God has prepared for those who love Him."(1
Corinthians 1:9)

Single Mom in Christ

The three single mothers in this book have allowed me to form an ironclad faith that God loves single mothers and in the absence of an earthly husband will step in and fulfill the role. Even though these women lived a few millennia ago, their struggles and challenges are very recognizable to those of us on the single mom journey today. Single mothers today continue to contend with the same range of issues that our predecessors had, from feeling isolated and alone to worrying about our children's future. No matter what, the issue, the consistent lesson from these women has been that once we submit to the Lord, seemingly impossible obstacles are resolved.

The Lord does not "leave us as orphans" as it states in John 14:8, through His love letter to us—the Bible—He interjects a solution to every problem humanity has created for itself. In using the word "problem," I don't mean that single motherhood is a problem, but it's not the ideal. Children are best raised in a home where two loving parents are following the Lord. When this is not available and not the case, the Lord wants us to know that He is there for us.

> The LORD is my rock and my fortress and my deliverer, My God, my rock, in whom I take refuge; My shield and the horn of my salvation, my stronghold. (Psalm 18:2 NIV)

In studying the single mothers of the Bible, it has been demonstrated that the Lord is indeed a father to the fatherless and a husband when none is available. Like an earthly father and husband in these stories, the Lord has been a protector, companion, and provider. Hagar experienced Him as both the "God, who sees me" and "the God, who hears." A good husband pays attention and listens. In keeping with the duties of a husband the Lord provided for every woman and child featured. They all received the physical elements that were needed for daily life.

In the role of father and protector, God made sure that not one of the young men entrusted to His care came to a disastrous end. He rescued the two boys from falling into a life of bondage. He gave them hope and a future. Much like the fathers of ancient times when Ishmael was on the threshold of adulthood God pronounced a blessing upon him setting him on a path to success. The Lord spoke about Ishmael's promising future, his family and a long line of descendants.

Once again it bears mentioning that our God is a person of eternal perspective, and it is not by accident that each of the stories we read held an aspect of a child at risk. The Lord stepped in and rescued each and every child. He was sure to demonstrate that He is the author of life and fully in control, not statistics, people or situations. What God did in the lives of the children from Biblical single parent households provides us today with an assurance that our children are safe in His hands. Impossible situations do not exist for our God. Our offspring are due full and satisfying futures as long as we submit them to the care and influence of the Lord. In fact, Jesus Christ in John 10:10 proclaims that He has come to provide an abundant and satisfying life.

> The thief's purpose is to steal and kill and destroy. My purpose is to give them a rich and satisfying life. (John 10:10 NLT)

The satisfying life mentioned above is not only for the benefit of our children, but it also extends to us as well. The Lord can truly be our provider, companion, and father to our children if we only turn to Him and let go of anything that would put a barrier between Him and us. We saw that in every instance a woman relinquished her control over her finances, meager resources, or the lives of her children, the Lord stepped up to the plate with magnificent flare. His interactions with these single mothers have given me an assurance that has transformed my life. I now know without a shadow of a doubt that the Lord loves my child and me, and He is there for us through the entire journey. I understand that even though I am a single mother, I can be used mightily by God to help whomever He may set up for a divine appointment. More importantly, I can hold my head up high in whatever circumstance because I am not alone. I have as a husband and partner who happens to be the Maker of the Universe.

If that were not enough, single mothers today have one advantage that our predecessors lacked. With the coming of the Lord Jesus Christ, we have the ability to receive the Holy Spirit, who will be there with us every waking moment. We can confidently ask the Lord to walk with us and help us to make decisions, take our children to and from school, and give us an even deeper and more intimate fellowship with God. When we add it all together, one thing is crystal clear: God loves us and will walk with us through the single mom journey.

ABOUT THE AUTHOR

Stephane Paul is the mother of one young man. Throughout her single mom experience, she has made it a point to be involved in the PTA and parent organizations to not only serve as an advocate for her child but look after the interests of children at large. In her spare time, she has written articles for trade magazines and co-produced a column suggesting books to entice young readers.

54585231R00066

Made in the USA
Lexington, KY
21 August 2016